Sight Word Tales™

Who Would Buy These Clothes?

by Catherine Bittner
illustrated by Richard Torrey

SCHOLASTIC INC.
New York • Toronto • London • Auckland • Sydney
Mexico City • New Delhi • Hong Kong • Buenos Aires

Designed by Maria Lilja
ISBN-13: 978-0-545-01668-1 • ISBN-10: 0-545-01668-1

First printing, January 2008

12 11 10 9 8 7 6 5 4 3 11 12 13/0

Sight Words

Sight words are words that you see again and again when you read. This book is filled with the sight words **who**, **would**, **these**, and **funny**. Look for them in the text. Check the pictures, too!

Look at **these**! Look at those!
Who would buy **these funny** clothes?

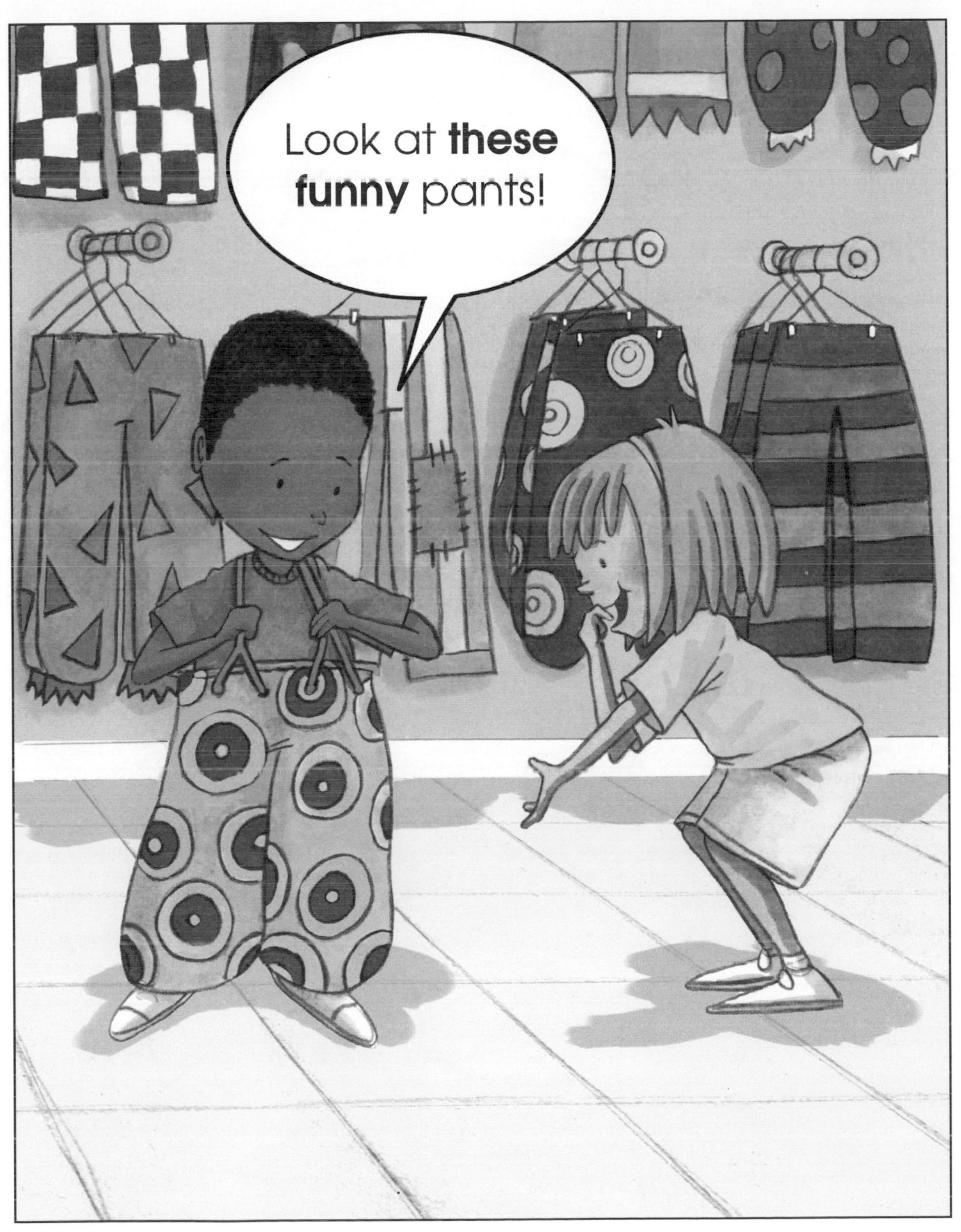

Who would buy **these funny** pants?

Who would buy **these funny** shirts?

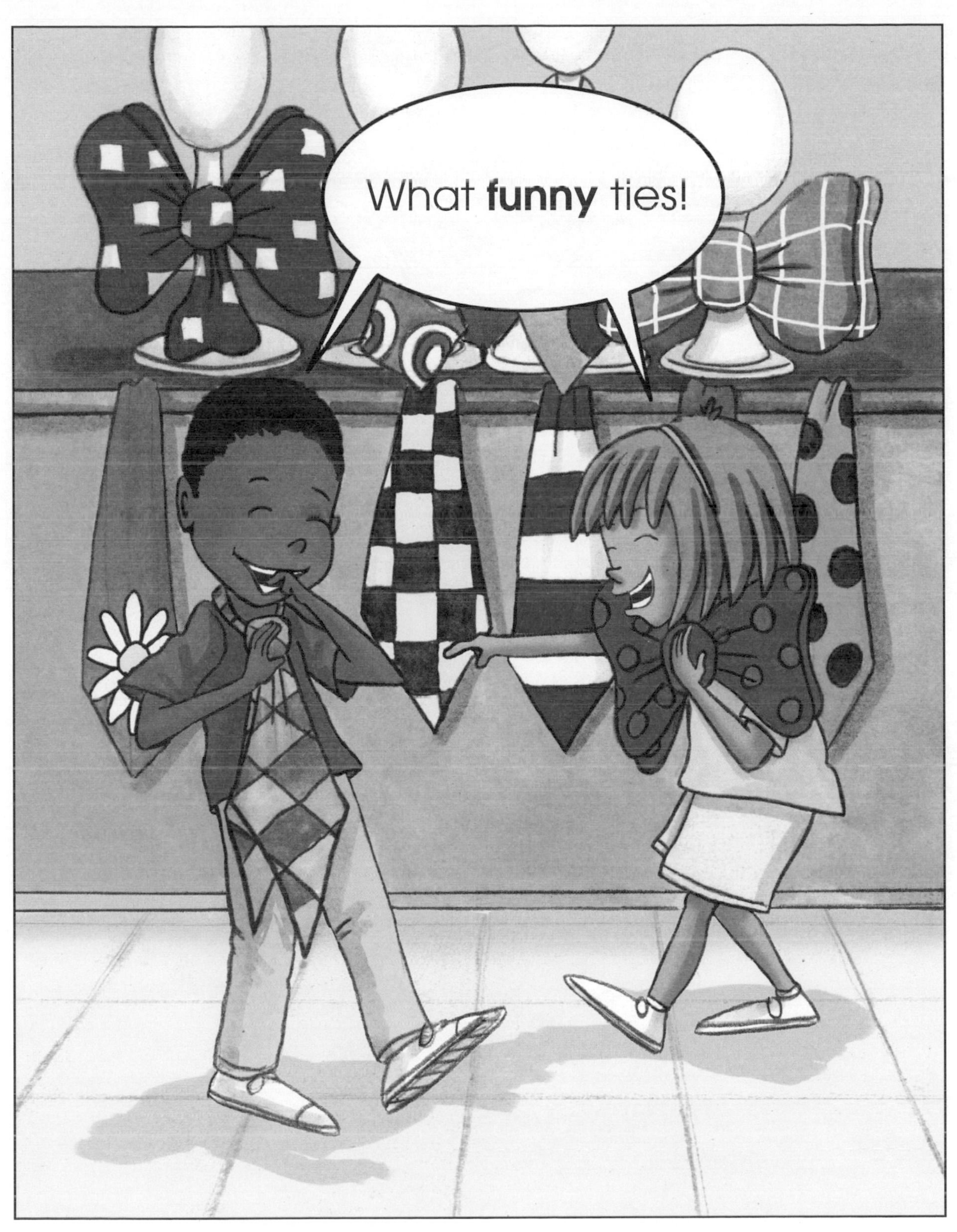

Who would buy **these funny** ties?

Who would buy **these funny** skirts?

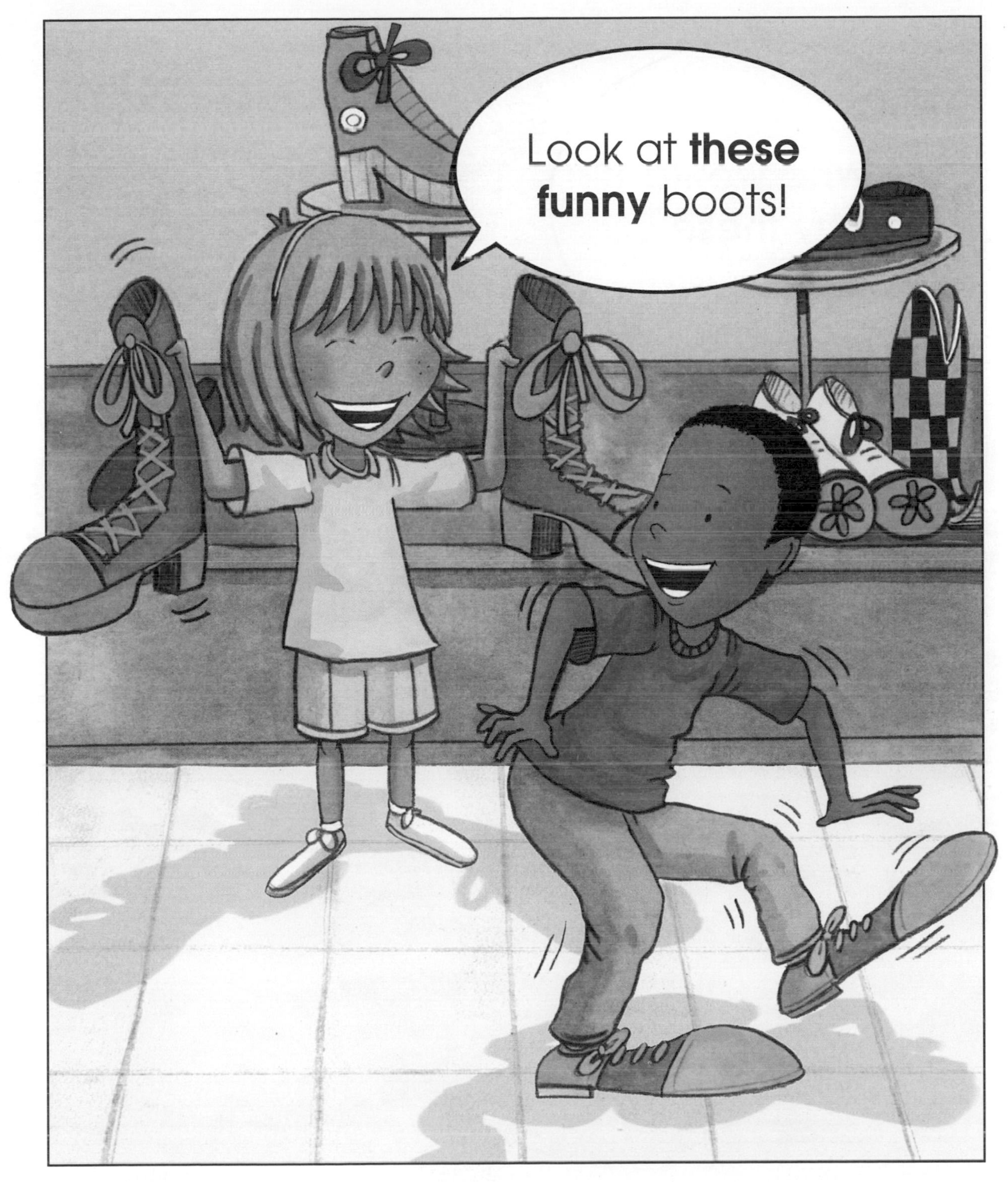

Who would buy **these funny** shoes?
Who would buy **these funny** boots?

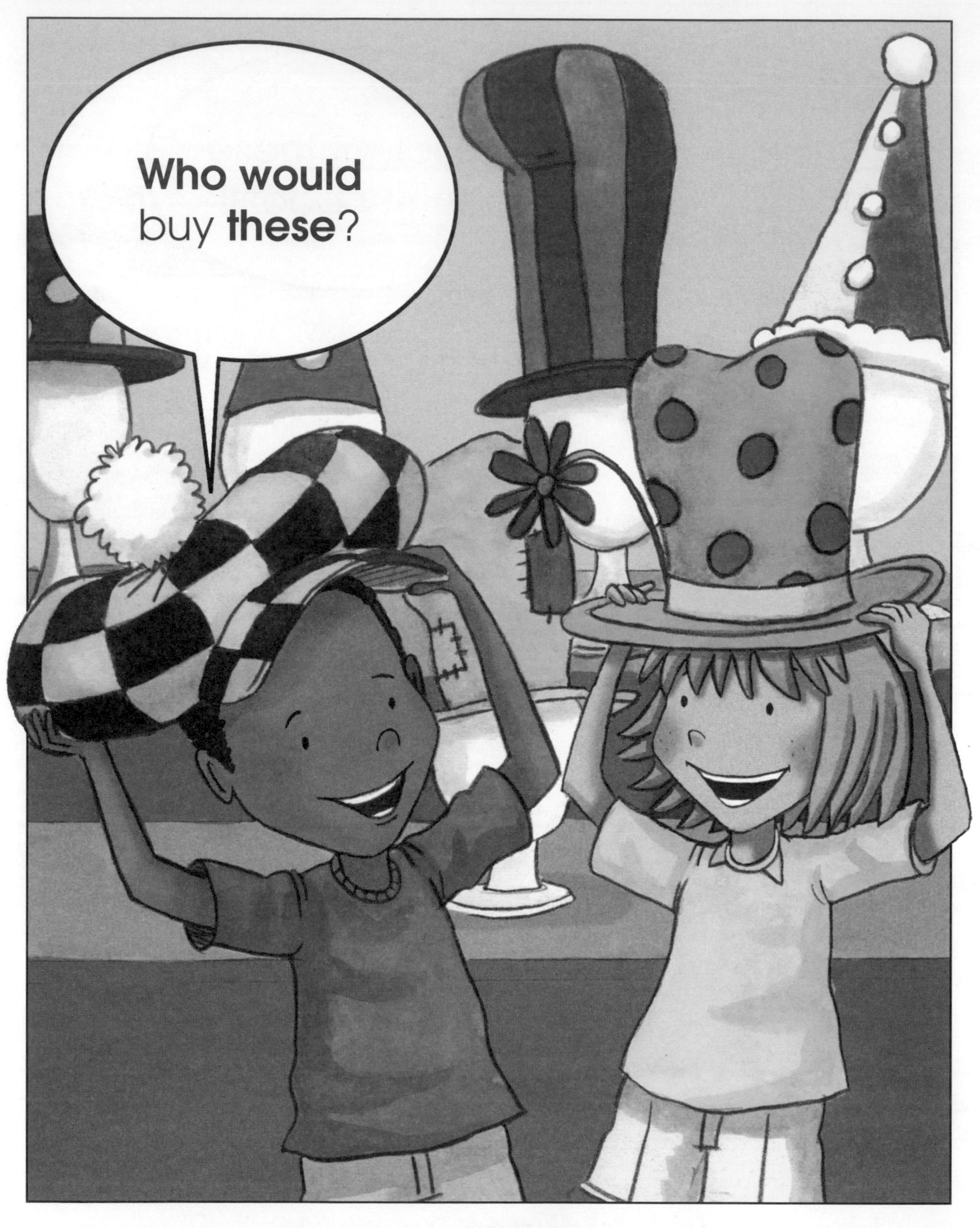

Who would buy **these funny** hats?

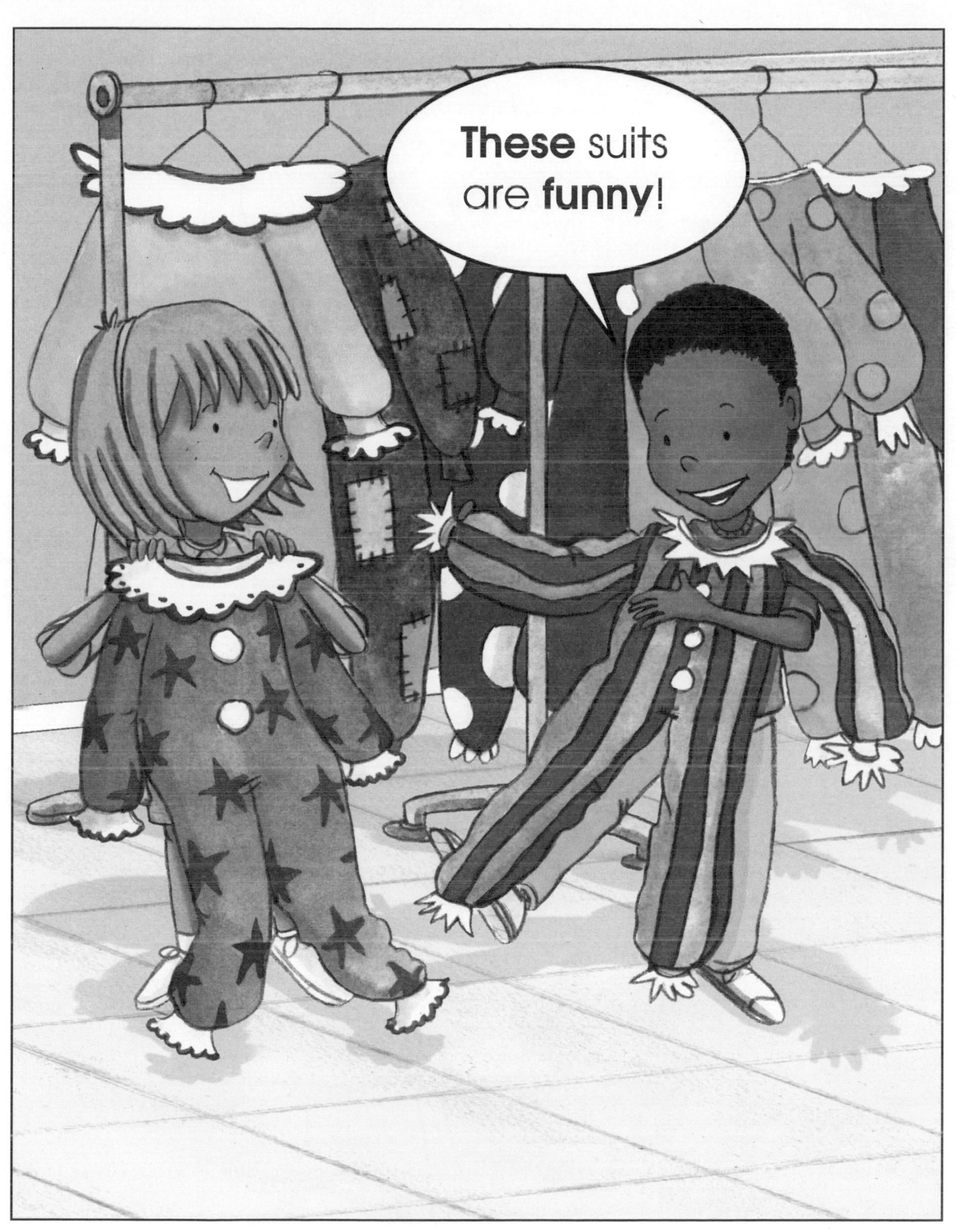

Who would buy **these funny** suits?

Who would buy **these funny** wigs?

Who would buy **these funny** gowns?

Oh! That's **who would** buy **these funny** clothes. . .

clowns!

Sight Word Review

who would
these funny

Do you know the four sight words in this book? Read aloud the word on each hat.

Sight Word Fill-ins

who would
these funny

Listen to the sentences. Then choose a sight word from the box to fill in each blank.

Word Box	who	would	these	funny

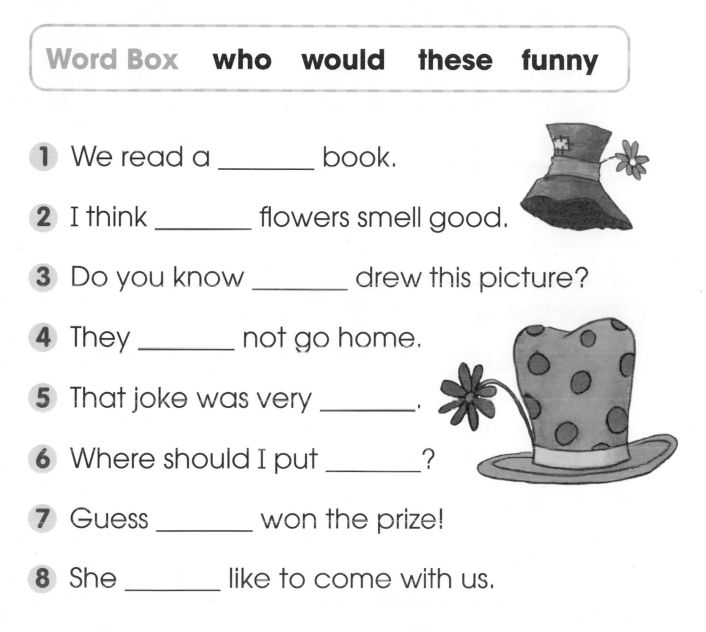

1. We read a _______ book.
2. I think _______ flowers smell good.
3. Do you know _______ drew this picture?
4. They _______ not go home.
5. That joke was very _______.
6. Where should I put _______?

7. Guess _______ won the prize!
8. She _______ like to come with us.

Answers: 1. funny 2. these 3. who 4. would 5. funny 6. these 7. who 8. would

Sight Word Cheers

who would
these funny

Celebrate the new sight words you learned by saying these four short cheers.

W-h-o! Give a yell!
What do these three letters spell?
A sight word that we all know well —
Who, who, who!

W-o-u-l-d! Give a yell!
What do these five letters spell?
A sight word that we all know well —
Would, would, would!

T-h-e-s-e! Give a yell!
What do these five letters spell?
A sight word that we all know well —
These, these, these!

F-u-n-n-y! Give a yell!
What do these five letters spell?
A sight word that we all know well —
Funny, funny, funny!